D1278109

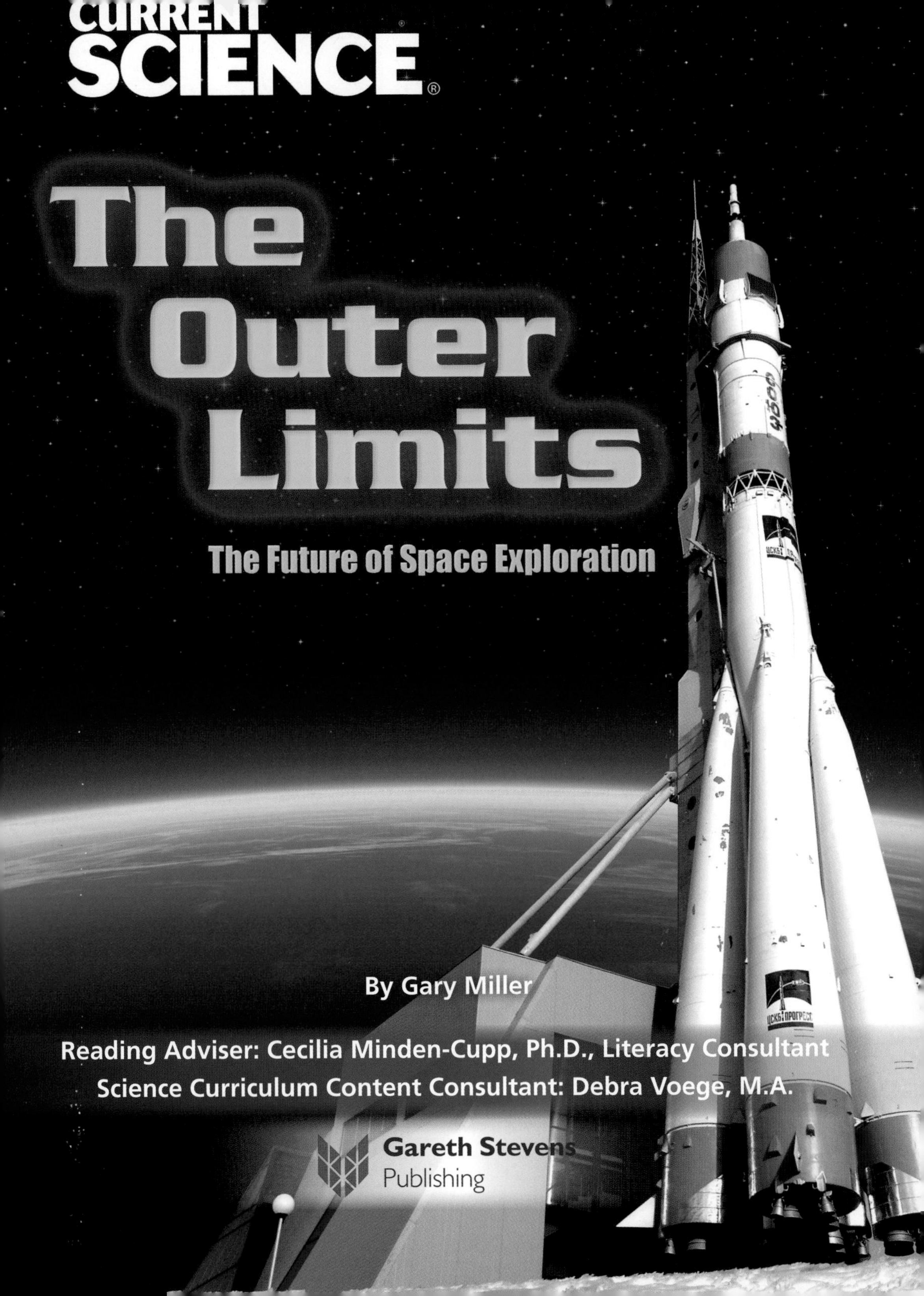

CURRENT SCIENCE®

The Outer Limits

The Future of Space Exploration

By Gary Miller

Reading Adviser: Cecilia Minden-Cupp, Ph.D., Literacy Consultant
Science Curriculum Content Consultant: Debra Voege, M.A.

Gareth Stevens
Publishing

For a free color catalog describing Gareth Stevens Publishing's list of high-quality books, call 1-800-542-2595 (USA) or 1-800-387-3178 (Canada). Gareth Stevens Publishing's fax: 1-877-542-2596

Library of Congress Cataloging-in-Publication Data

Miller, Gary.
      Outer limits : the future of space exploration / by Gary Miller ; reading specialist, Cecilia Minden ; science curriculum content consultant, Debra Voege.
         p. cm. — (Current science)
      Includes bibliographical references and index.
      ISBN-10: 1-4339-2242-8   ISBN-13: 978-1-4339-2242-8 (lib. bdg.)
      1. Space flight—Juvenile literature. 2. Outer space—Exploration—Juvenile literature. 3. Astronautics—Juvenile literature. I. Title.
      TL793.M548   2010
      629.4'1—dc22
                                     2009006214

This edition first published in 2010 by
Gareth Stevens Publishing
A Weekly Reader® Company
1 Reader's Digest Road
Pleasantville, NY 10570-7000 USA

Current Science™ is a trademark of Weekly Reader Corporation. Used under license.

Gareth Stevens Executive Managing Editor: Lisa M. Herrington
Gareth Stevens Senior Editor: Barbara Bakowski
Gareth Stevens Cover Designer: Keith Plechaty

Created by **Q2AMedia**
Editor: Jessica Cohn
Art Director: Rahul Dhiman
Designer: Harleen Mehta
Photo Researcher: Kamal Kumar
Illustrators: Ashish Tanwar, Indranil Ganguly, Kusum Kala, Nazia Zaidi, Rohit Sharma

Printed in the United States of America

1 2 3 4 5 6 7 8 9 12 11 10 09

CONTENTS

Words in **boldface** type are defined in the glossary.

Chapter 1

Rocket TO THE FUTURE

Ten . . . nine . . . eight . . . seven . . . six . . . five . . . four . . . three . . . two . . . one . . . LIFTOFF!

The first rocket blasted off into space in the 1950s. Today, our dreams of space exploration are even bigger. We are preparing to build a base on the Moon. We are also getting ready for a voyage to Mars.

Star systems are called **galaxies**.

DREAMS TO GO

Humans have been dreaming of worlds beyond Earth for a long time. Ancient Egyptians practiced **astronomy**, the study of stars and planets. Ancient Greeks and Romans looked into the night sky and gave names to the **constellations**. Constellations are the groups of stars that form patterns we can recognize. The ancient Greeks thought quite a bit about the dangers of the sky, too. For instance, one famous ancient Greek story is about Icarus. In the story, Icarus tried to fly. He used wings made from feathers and wax. Icarus flew too close to the Sun. The wax melted. Icarus fell into the sea and drowned.

Real-life **astronauts** face dangers ancient people could not have imagined. Why do these space travelers do it? They want to satisfy their taste for adventure. They want to learn more about space. The astronauts want to understand our own planet better. They also want to answer the biggest question of all: Does life exist on other worlds?

New adventures in space might answer that question. Fasten your seat belts. Get ready for a trip to the outer limits!

FIRST SATELLITE

On October 4, 1957, scientists launched the first artificial **satellite**. A satellite is an object that **orbits** Earth or another body in space. *Orbit* means "to travel around." The tiny satellite was called *Sputnik 1*. It was launched by the former Soviet Union. The Soviet Union was a nation that included Russia and many other territories.

John Glenn was the first U.S. astronaut to orbit Earth.

THE SPACE RACE

In response to the Sputnik program, the United States started a space program of its own. The National Aeronautics and Space Administration (NASA) was created. In early 1958, NASA launched its first satellite. The Space Race had begun!

Since then, rockets have carried people into space. Humans have walked on the Moon. Nations are working together on a **space station**, an international laboratory that orbits Earth.

FAST FACT
Space begins at about 62 miles (100 kilometers) above Earth's surface.

When rockets reach a certain height, the bottom sections fall to Earth.

The Race to Space

1958
NASA launches *Explorer 1*, the first U.S. satellite.

1957
The Soviet Union launches *Sputnik 1*.

1961
Yuri Gagarin of the Soviet Union becomes the first human in space.

1962
John Glenn becomes the first American to orbit Earth.

1977
NASA launches space probes *Voyager 1* and *Voyager 2*.

1969
The **crew** of *Apollo 11* makes the first Moon landing.

1981
The first passengers orbit Earth in the **space shuttle** *Columbia*.

1983
Sally Ride becomes the first American woman in space.

2000
The first residents board *Alpha*, the International Space Station.

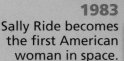

2004
The rover *Spirit* lands on Mars.

2008
Voyager 1 reaches the edge of the **solar system**.

FIRST TO THE MOON

On May 25, 1961, President John F. Kennedy announced the new mission of the Apollo space program. The program's goal was to put a human on the Moon. On July 20, 1969, the program reached its goal. Take a look at some key Apollo missions.

- *Apollo 1*, January 27, 1967: The first Apollo mission ended in disaster. A fire on the **launchpad** killed three astronauts—Virgil Grissom, Edward White, and Roger Chaffee.

- *Apollo 7*, October 11–22, 1968: Three astronauts orbited Earth 163 times. They became the first to "splash down" for an ocean landing.

- *Apollo 8*, December 21–27, 1968: The astronauts aboard *Apollo 8* became the first humans to orbit the Moon and return to Earth.

- *Apollo 9*, March 3–13, 1969: This mission was the first to carry the **lunar module** into space. The lunar module was the vehicle that would land on the Moon's surface with the astronauts inside.

- *Apollo 10*, May 18–26, 1969: This flight was a test run for a full Moon mission. The lunar module separated from the rest of the spacecraft. The lunar module orbited the Moon. Then it docked, or reconnected, with the rest of the spacecraft.

- *Apollo 11*, July 16–24, 1969: The Apollo program is a full success! On July 20, 1969, Neil Armstrong became the first human to walk on the Moon.

In 1969, Neil Armstrong planted a U.S. flag on the Moon.

Lunar Log Book

THE MOON'S AGE: Approximately 4 billion years

ORIGIN: A Mars-sized body collided with Earth. The Moon was formed from the resulting **debris**.

SURFACE: Rock, covered with huge **craters** caused by collisions with other objects

WATER: None

GRAVITY: About 17 percent of Earth's **gravity**. If you weigh 100 pounds (45.4 kilograms) on Earth, you would weigh 17 pounds (7.7 kg) on the Moon.

MAXIMUM TEMPERATURES: About 253 degrees Fahrenheit (123 degrees Celsius) day; -387 degrees F (-233 degrees C) night

The *Apollo 9* lunar module had stairs for the astronauts.

NEXT ACT

What is next for Earth's brave explorers? NASA has all kinds of plans. Yet two major efforts stand out. One is a return to the Moon. The other mission will send people to Mars!

BACK TO THE MOON

Our first missions to the Moon were short. The longest lasted only 75 hours. Now NASA plans to build a base on the Moon. The new Moon base would include laboratories and living quarters. Scientists would use the Moon base as a place to study space. The Moon base would also be a training ground for astronauts. There, the space explorers could prepare for the first voyage to another planet.

Only 59 percent of the Moon is visible from Earth.

More Nations Race Into Space

The year 2008 was a big one for international "firsts" in space. India's first unmanned mission reached the Moon's orbit. Japanese astronaut Takao Doi made a voyage to the International Space Station. Finally, Zhai Zhigang became the first Chinese astronaut to walk in space. Jing Haipeng, Zhai Zhigang, and Liu Boming (shown from left to right) became heroes in China after their successful space mission.

LIFE ON MARS?

Why send humans to Mars? One reason is the search for life. No other planet has a climate that can support life. Venus's surface temperature is 870 degrees F (465 degrees C). The temperature in Uranus's **atmosphere** is -355 degrees F (-215 degrees C). *Brr!*

Temperatures on the surface of Mars average -80 degrees F (-60 degrees C). That is awfully cold for humans, but not too cold to support life. Mars also has ice on its surface. The presence of ice means liquid water could be found. All known life-forms need liquid water to survive.

Mars is smaller than Earth but has about the same amount of land. More than 70 percent of Earth's surface is covered in water.

Chapter 2

Distances and Dangers

What does it take to go to the Moon or to Mars? It is one thing to launch a spacecraft with no people. Spacecraft are complicated machines, yet they are simply tools. They fly off and get jobs done. Some upcoming missions, however, will put people in danger.

↑ MOON
239,000 MILES
(384,000 KM)

EXPLORERS THEN AND NOW

In 1492, Christopher Columbus set sail from Spain. He wanted to find a new route to trading lands in Asia. Columbus and his crew sailed for more than two months. Finally, they reached land in the Americas.

Sea travel was dangerous then. Huge storms could damage ships and even sink them. Ships carried limited supplies of food and water. Disease could strike at any time. Worst, perhaps, was the isolation felt by the crew. The sailors were on their own.

Future space explorers will travel great distances into unknown territory. They will pilot small ships that hold limited supplies. The explorers will visit harsh climates. They will face fear, boredom, and probably disease. Space scientists on Earth will provide them with support. Yet deep in space, the explorers will be completely alone.

Strange but True

The Moon is, on average, about 239,000 miles (384,000 km) from Earth. How long would it take to drive to the Moon? If you drove at 65 miles (105 km) per hour, your trip would take about 152 days. That is without stopping for a bathroom break!

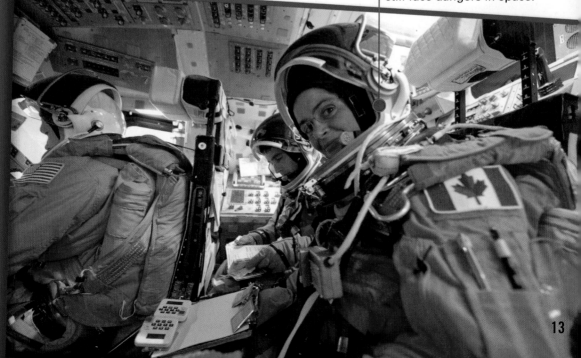

Although today's explorers have high-tech tools, they still face dangers in space.

CS INFOGRAPHIC

Road Map to SPACE

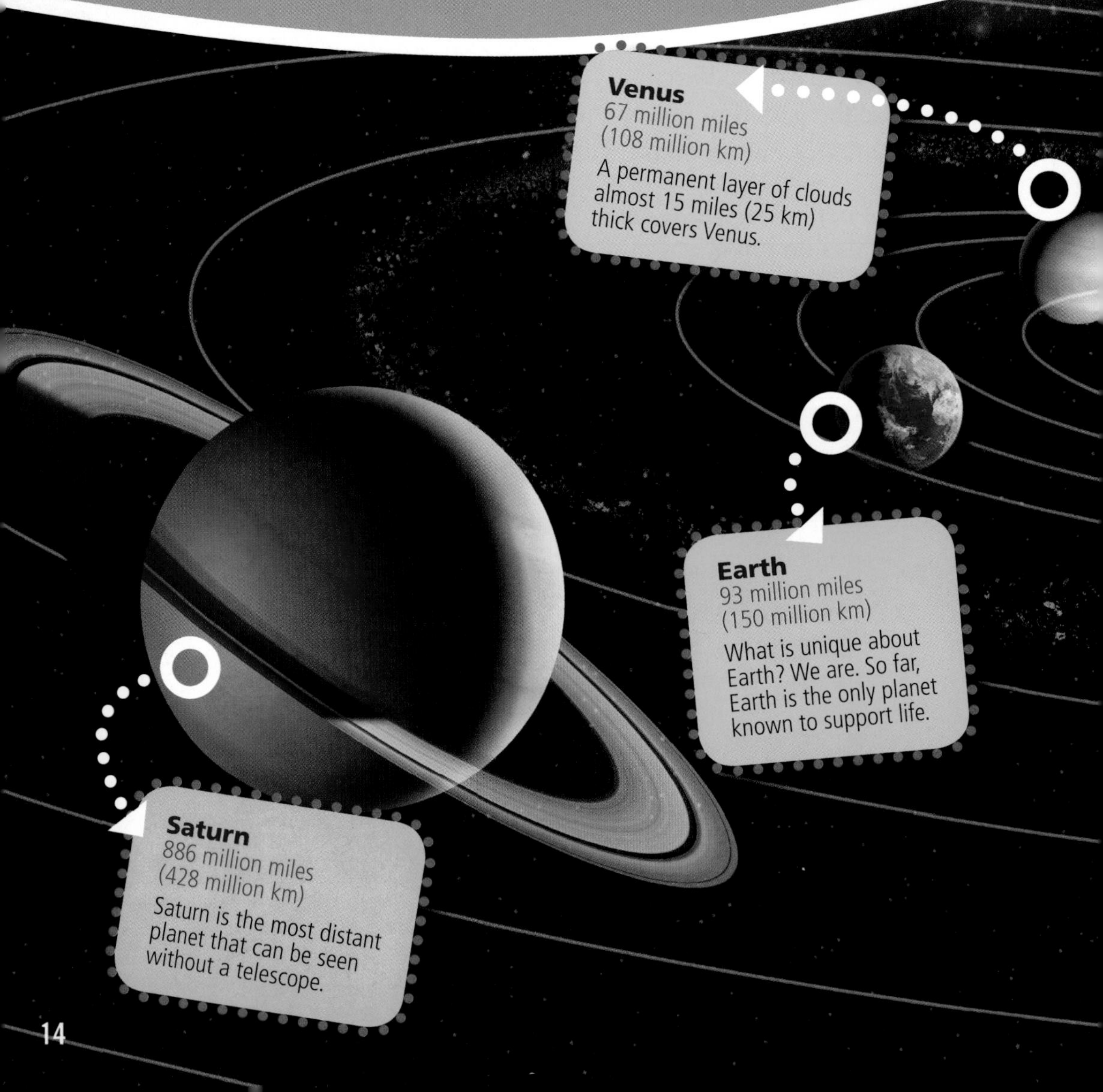

Venus
67 million miles
(108 million km)

A permanent layer of clouds almost 15 miles (25 km) thick covers Venus.

Earth
93 million miles
(150 million km)

What is unique about Earth? We are. So far, Earth is the only planet known to support life.

Saturn
886 million miles
(428 million km)

Saturn is the most distant planet that can be seen without a telescope.

The star known as the Sun is at the center of our solar system. How far from this star are the planets?

Pluto: What's in a Name?
From its discovery in 1930 until 2006, tiny Pluto was known as a planet. Today, Pluto is known as a dwarf planet. NASA plans to explore it in 2015.

Neptune
2.8 billion miles (4.5 billion km)
Neptune was named for the Roman god of the sea.

Uranus
1.8 billion miles (2.9 billion km)
Uranus has no solid surface. It is mostly made up of gases.

Mars
141 million miles (227 million km)
A mineral called iron oxide gives the soil on Mars its red color.

Sun

Mercury
36 million miles (58 million km)
Mercury orbits the Sun about once every 88 days.

Jupiter
483 million miles (779 million km)
Jupiter has 16 known moons. Three of them are bigger than Earth's Moon.

ROCKET SCIENCE

Take a baseball. Throw it as high as you can into the air. That takes a lot of arm power. Now imagine throwing a spacecraft and a crew into space!

Rockets provide the power to lift spacecraft off Earth's surface. How can rockets do this? Liquid or solid **propellant**, or fuel, is burned inside a rocket. Hot gases from the fire shoot out through a nozzle. The pressure of the gases makes the rocket move.

AN EXPLOSIVE HISTORY

Chinese soldiers were using simple rockets as weapons as early as the year 1200. The soldiers attached a tube of gunpowder to an arrow to create a flying arrow of fire. For hundreds of years, rockets were used mostly in warfare. By the late 1800s, inventors had come up with other uses of rockets—delivering mail, for example! At the end of the 19th century, though, people were beginning to connect rockets with the idea of space travel.

In 1926, Robert H. Goddard launched the first liquid-fueled rocket. His rocket flew for only 2.5 seconds. It landed 184 feet (56 meters) away in a cabbage patch. That achievement, however, marked the beginning of a technology that would later take humans into space.

Robert Goddard: Rocket Man

In 1899, a boy named Robert Goddard read a **science fiction** novel called *War of the Worlds*. Science fiction stories imagine the impact of technology on the future. *War of the Worlds* describes a **Martian** invasion of Earth. The book inspired Goddard to build a machine that could fly into space.

In 1926, Goddard launched the first "modern" rocket. His launchpad was his Aunt Effie's farm. Later, Goddard designed a rocket steering system. He helped improve rocket engines, too. His work helped pave the way for future rocket builders.

Rocket Roundup

Here are just a few of the many rockets used to send people and objects into space.

Rocket	Maker	Size	Sample Mission
A Class	Soviet Union	98 feet (29 m)	Launched *Sputnik 1*; carried Yuri Gagarin, first man in space
Jupiter C	United States	71 feet (22 m)	Launched first U.S. satellite, *Explorer 1*
Mercury–Redstone	United States	83 feet (25 m)	Launched Alan Shepard, first American in space
Saturn 5	United States	363 feet (111 m)	Launched crew of *Apollo 11* to first Moon landing
Space Shuttle	United States	189 feet (56 m)	Traveled to the International Space Station

ADVENTURERS AT RISK

It was January 28, 1986. The space shuttle *Challenger* roared into the sky. Christa McAuliffe, a teacher from New Hampshire, was aboard as part of NASA's Teacher in Space project. Just 73 seconds after takeoff, *Challenger* exploded. All seven crew members lost their lives. Billions of people saw the explosion on television. They could not believe what they had seen. The explosion was one of the most tragic events in the history of space exploration. Space exploration had always been risky. Yet this was an event that brought the message home.

The *Challenger* crew lost their lives when the shuttle exploded in 1986. Christa McAuliffe (back, second from left) was to be the first Teacher in Space.

SUITED FOR DANGER

Stepping into space is risky. Spacesuits help keep astronauts safe.

Spacesuits have tanks that provide breathable air.

To combat temperature extremes, the helmet is made of protective material.

Tough fabrics protect astronauts from debris.

The Sun's **radiation** could "cook" a person. The suit's materials protect the skin.

Space explorers are outfitted with tools to make fast repairs as needed.

19

YOU DO IT!

Shield "Astronauts" From Radiation

What You Need
- cardboard
- wire
- UV beads (available at craft stores)

What You Do

Step 1
Count out four UV beads. These beads change color to detect solar radiation. They represent astronauts.

Step 2
Build a cardboard spacecraft. Put two UV bead astronauts inside. Attach the other two astronauts to the outside of the spacecraft with wire.

Step 3
Take your spacecraft outside into the sunlight. Carry it around for a while. Which astronauts get the most radiation?

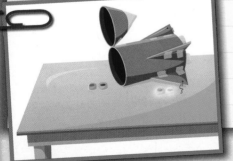

What Happened?
You can see why spacesuits must be specially designed.

Some astronaut training occurs underwater.

THE RIGHT STUFF

How do NASA astronauts prepare for dangerous missions? They undergo some of the most thorough training on Earth.

Candidates must meet certain requirements. Pilot and commander candidates must have at least 1,000 hours' experience as a jet pilot. They must have a degree in **engineering**, **biology**, **physics**, or mathematics. Mission specialist candidates need degrees, too. They also need work experience in the science field.

Astronaut training lasts from one to two years. How do trainees prepare? They study **geology**, astronomy, and many other topics. They learn land and sea survival skills. They even become trained scuba divers.

Trainees use **flight simulators** to practice launching, flying, and landing a spacecraft. Simulators let astronauts experience the challenges of spaceflight without the risks.

Chapter 3

Return to the Moon

What is next in space exploration? NASA is preparing for a return to the Moon in the next decade. Crews will build a permanent base there. NASA is working on new spacecraft to bring astronauts back to the Moon—and maybe beyond.

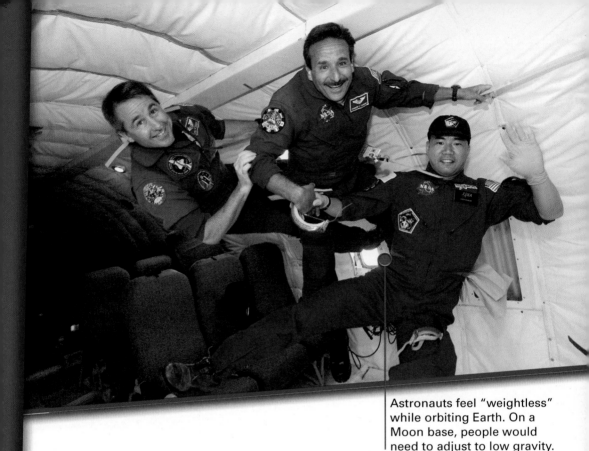

Astronauts feel "weightless" while orbiting Earth. On a Moon base, people would need to adjust to low gravity.

BASE OF OPERATION

Building a Moon base will be neither easy nor cheap. Why do it? The most important reason is research. The Moon offers clues about the time when the planets were formed.

A Moon base may also help with some of our energy needs on Earth. The Moon gets lots of solar radiation. Someday, we might build solar power stations on the Moon.

Going to and living on the Moon are stepping stones to future exploration. A Moon base could also support other space missions. The Moon is more like Mars than Earth is.

So the Moon would be a great testing ground for a Mars mission. The Moon would make a good launchpad, too.

WHAT DO YOU THINK?

Would you want to be an astronaut on the first Moon base? Why or why not?

23

PREPARING FOR THE MISSION

Preparing for a Moon mission will not be easy. Fortunately, NASA already has valuable tools that can help with the new project.

THE INTERNATIONAL SPACE STATION

The International Space Station has been orbiting Earth since 1998. The space station is an important means for learning how to live in space. It will be helpful as human space travel pushes farther beyond Earth.

For more than 10 years, the space station was under construction in orbit. Rockets launched pieces of the station into space. Astronauts put the pieces together. The project required the efforts of 16 nations.

Shuttles carried astronauts and supplies to the space station. Shuttle crews carried out needed repairs in space. The date of the last official mission for the U.S. shuttle fleet was 2010. Yet space station research continued.

Research in the station's labs benefits people all over the world. Experiments in medicine could lead to possible treatments for cancer and other diseases. Another area of research is the effects of low gravity on humans. An understanding of those effects will help NASA prepare for future human exploration of the Moon and beyond.

The space station has been assembled piece by piece.

FAST FACT
Once completed, the space station will be about the size of a five-bedroom house.

Eeew! Space Garbage!

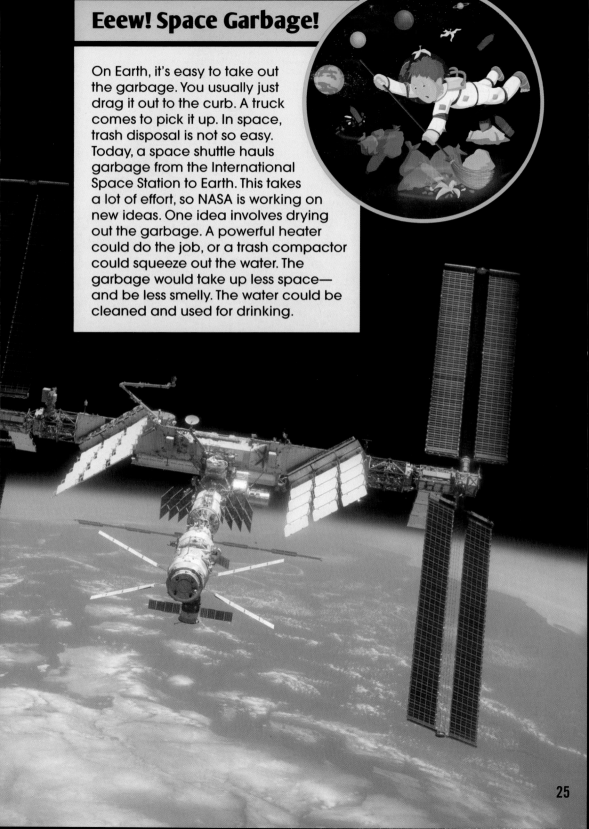

On Earth, it's easy to take out the garbage. You usually just drag it out to the curb. A truck comes to pick it up. In space, trash disposal is not so easy. Today, a space shuttle hauls garbage from the International Space Station to Earth. This takes a lot of effort, so NASA is working on new ideas. One idea involves drying out the garbage. A powerful heater could do the job, or a trash compactor could squeeze out the water. The garbage would take up less space— and be less smelly. The water could be cleaned and used for drinking.

WHAT DO YOU THINK?

What might be some of the challenges involved in building new spacecraft?

The inside of the *Orion* exploration vehicle will look like this.

LANDING GEAR

NASA is hard at work designing new spacecraft for the new challenges. These vehicles will help make the journey to the Moon safe and productive.

THE *ORION* CREW EXPLORATION VEHICLE

This spacecraft will fly its first mission to the Moon in 2020. *Orion* will be 16.5 feet (5 m) in diameter. It will weigh 25 tons (22.7 metric tons). *Orion* will be able to carry four astronauts to the Moon.

FAST FACT
How did the Moon-bound craft get their names? In Greek myth, Orion is a giant. Ares is the Greek god of war.

ARES AND ALTAIR

The *Ares I* rocket will carry *Orion* and its crew into orbit. The more powerful *Ares V* will carry the lunar landing vehicle into orbit. Once in space, *Orion* and the lunar landing vehicle will link up. A smaller rocket will launch the combined vehicle toward the Moon.

Altair will carry astronauts to the Moon's surface. It will bring enough supplies for a one-week stay. When the Moon mission ends, *Altair* will carry the crew back into space. With the astronauts back inside *Orion*, the spacecraft will break out of the Moon's orbit and head home to Earth.

An artist shows the *Altair* lunar lander on the Moon's surface.

Ares rockets will deliver *Orion* and *Altair* into space.

Prizes are being offered for the best space elevator design.

SPACE ELEVATOR, GOING UP!

Wouldn't it be nice if astronauts could simply take an elevator into space? This is not possible today, but someday it might be. Engineers are working to make it happen.

RIDING UP THE CABLE

How would the **space elevator** work? A long cable anchored to Earth would reach into orbit. It would be held in place by a satellite. Loads of cargo—and maybe even people—would ride the elevator. At the top of the cable, cargo would be loaded onto spacecraft. People could hop on, too. Then a rocket would launch the spacecraft deeper into space.

How could a space elevator cable stay in place? One reason is **inertia**. Inertia means that an object resists a change in its state of motion. A moving object keeps moving unless something slows it down. A still object stays still unless something makes it move. Inertia would keep the cable tightly stretched.

MONEY SAVER

Powerful rockets are needed to launch vehicles and crews into space. Those rockets cost a lot of money. Spaceflight is expensive. In 2008, it cost about $10,000 to launch just 1 pound (0.45 kg) into space! A space elevator could do the job for a lot less money.

YOU DO IT!

Demonstrate Inertia

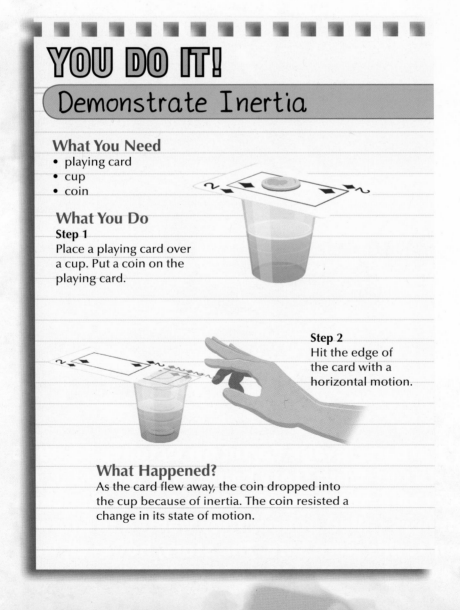

What You Need
- playing card
- cup
- coin

What You Do

Step 1
Place a playing card over a cup. Put a coin on the playing card.

Step 2
Hit the edge of the card with a horizontal motion.

What Happened?
As the card flew away, the coin dropped into the cup because of inertia. The coin resisted a change in its state of motion.

Chapter 4

Mars and BEYOND

Martians invade Earth! On October 30, 1938, a terrifying story came over the radio. A spaceship had landed in New Jersey. Panicked listeners called police. They wanted to know if their towns were safe. The story, however, was a radio play called *War of the Worlds*.

The Hubble Space Telescope took this close-up of the Red Planet.

MARTIAN CANALS

War of the Worlds is just one of many fictional stories about beings from Mars. The fascination with Mars started in 1877. Astronomer Giovanni Schiaparelli looked at Mars through a telescope. He thought he saw **canals** on the surface. Martians must have built the canals, he thought.

In 1971, the **space probe** *Mariner 9* orbited Mars. A probe is a spacecraft without a crew. *Mariner* took photographs of the dry, dusty surface. The photos showed huge volcanoes and deep canyons but no canals. Schiaparelli had been mistaken.

A Look at Telescopes

Early telescopes were small. They let people view space from the ground. In the 1600s, Galileo Galilei used telescopes to study the sky. He showed that our solar system is **heliocentric**—the planets go around the Sun. Modern telescopes see much farther and clearer. In 1990, NASA launched the Hubble Space Telescope into orbit around Earth. A new telescope, to launch in 2013, will orbit 1 million miles (1.6 million km) from home!

Rovers are built to ride over rough ground, like the surface of Mars.

DIGGING FOR MORE

Current and future Mars missions will reveal even more about the planet. Probes send images and information about Mars. Some probes deliver **rovers** and **landers** to explore the planet's surface. Rovers and landers are two kinds of robots sent to study a space object. Rovers travel on the surface.

Landers stay in one place. Rovers and landers take photographs and collect samples of rock and soil. The robots can even do some simple experiments.

In 2004, two rovers called *Spirit* and *Opportunity* landed on Mars. The rovers found signs that the planet was once wet.

A WATERY DISCOVERY

In 2008, the *Phoenix* Mars lander collected soil on Mars. The soil included tiny crystals of ice. Why is that discovery important? Proof of water on Mars could help scientists figure out whether the planet can support life.

WHAT DO YOU THINK?

What will be the most important discovery on Mars? How will that information be useful?

FAST FACT

Ice isn't the only cool feature on Mars. The planet is home to Olympus Mons, the largest volcano in the solar system.

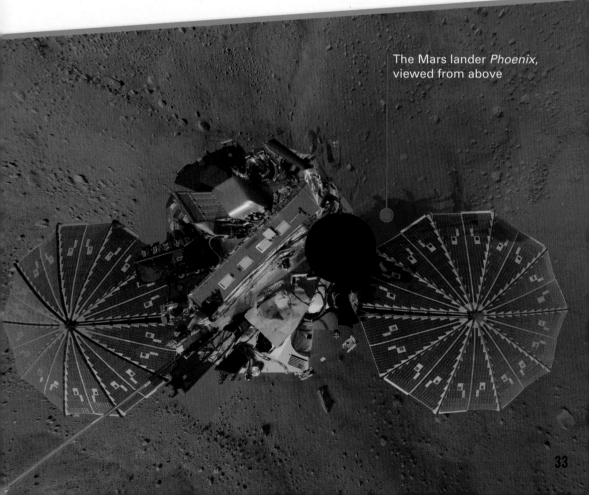

The Mars lander *Phoenix*, viewed from above

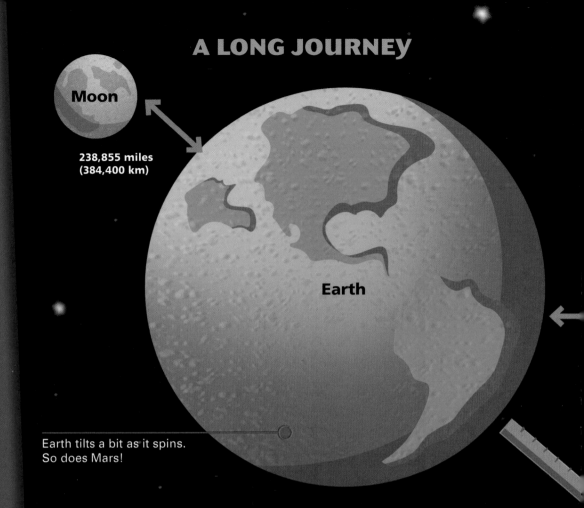

Moon

**238,855 miles
(384,400 km)**

Earth

Earth tilts a bit as it spins.
So does Mars!

ARE WE THERE YET?

Imagine a long car trip. The time passes slowly. You get bored. You want a change of scenery. You want to get out and stretch your legs. Now imagine a trip that lasts for months. You are trapped in a spacecraft with five other people.

You cannot even roll down the window. A spaceflight to Mars presents a huge challenge. The main reason is the distance. The distance between Mars and Earth depends on the planets' positions in their orbits. A voyage to Mars would probably take about 10 months.

FAST FACT
Earth passes Mars
once every 26 months
because Earth orbits
the Sun faster.

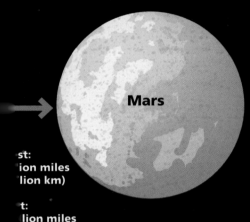

Mars

st:
ion miles
lion km)

t:
lion miles
llion km)

...MISSION

Getting astronauts to Mars and returning them safely to Earth is a challenging goal. The Mars mission will be difficult for astronauts. It is sure to cause physical problems. Life in low gravity can weaken muscles and bones. Long-term exposure to space radiation can cause disease. What if an astronaut gets sick? What if someone needs medicine or even surgery?

Space scientists are working hard to solve these problems. They are also working to find faster ways to get to Mars. One idea is to use new rockets. These rockets use a fuel called **plasma**. Plasma burns at an extremely high temperature. The new fuel could cut the journey to Mars to about four months.

FOR SALE

Strange but True

Some people are already buying and selling land on Mars. More than 2 million people have bought land there!

35

In 1989, the space shuttle *Atlantis* carried the *Galileo* probe into the sky. *Galileo* made a seven-year journey to the far reaches of the solar system. It studied Jupiter and its moons more closely. *Galileo* discovered that Jupiter has thunderstorms much larger than those on Earth. Jupiter's rings are made of small dust grains. Those grains were created when flying space objects hit and chipped Jupiter's moons. The icy moon Europa may have a salty ocean beneath its frozen surface. Another moon, named Io, has volcanoes hotter than any on Earth.

Cassini-Huygens launched in 1997. The spacecraft reached the ringed planet's orbit in 2004. *Cassini* orbited Titan, one of Saturn's moons. The *Huygens* probe landed on Titan and sent pictures back to Earth. Observations of Titan show what Earth might have been like long ago. Titan has many of the same features as Earth, including lakes, rivers, mountains, and possibly volcanoes. *Cassini* also explored another Saturn moon, the small, icy Enceladus. In 2008, *Cassini*'s mission was extended. NASA hopes to reveal more secrets of Saturn.

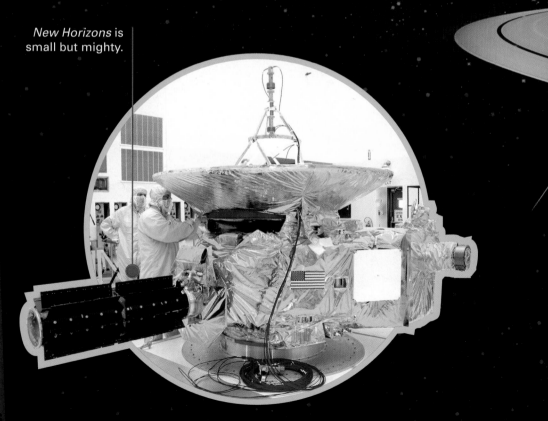

New Horizons is small but mighty.

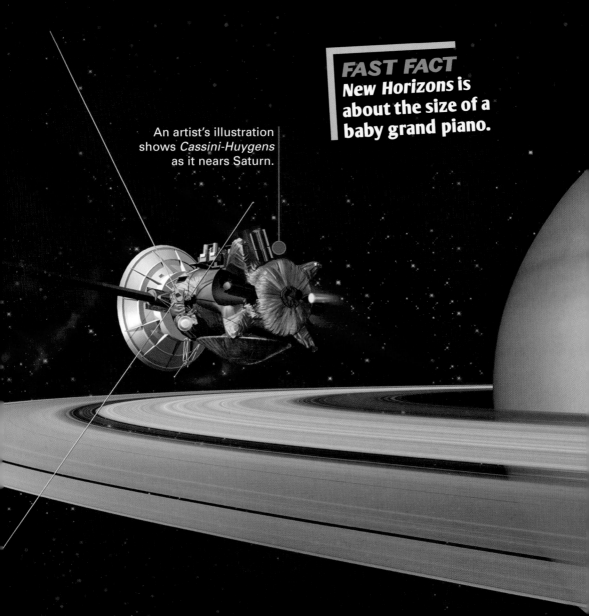

An artist's illustration
shows *Cassini-Huygens*
as it nears Saturn.

FAST FACT
New Horizons is
about the size of a
baby grand piano.

AT THE EDGE

In 2015, NASA's *New Horizons* spacecraft will make the first close-up study of Pluto and its three moons. Pluto is a dwarf planet at the edge of our solar system. It is 3 billion miles (4.8 billion km) from Earth!

New Horizons launched in 2006. After its Pluto **flyby**, the craft may go on to explore space beyond Pluto. The space agency is planning more missions to the outer planets. These voyages will set the stage for future research. They could answer questions about how our solar system formed. They could even find life elsewhere in the universe.

EXOPLANETS

The search for life beyond Earth has extended past Mars and into deep space. The universe is unbelievably vast. How can scientists narrow down the search? They can look at **exoplanets**. Exoplanets (short for "extrasolar planets") are planets beyond our solar system.

LIFE OUT THERE?

Is Earth one of a kind in our galaxy, which is called the Milky Way? If not, how many Earth-size planets might be orbiting stars in our galaxy?

In their search, scientists are looking for exoplanets similar to Earth. Some of these planets may contain water. They may also contain an atmosphere and a climate suitable for life.

Some exoplanets orbit very close to their stars.

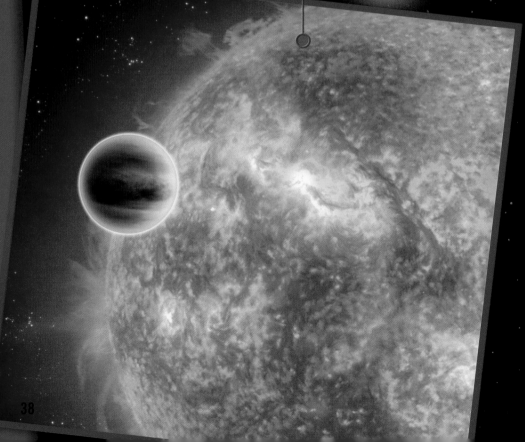

NASA's Kepler mission launched in 2009 to look for Earth-like planets in the Milky Way. It will tell scientists whether planets like ours are common. The Terrestrial Planet Finder is a possible future NASA project. It would study the formation and features of exoplanets.

In 2008, scientists photographed a massive planet. It appeared to be orbiting a star somewhat like our Sun. The planet was about 500 **light-years** from Earth. One light-year is the distance that light can travel in a single year. Light travels at a speed of 186,000 miles (298,000 km) per second. The planet in the photo is very far from Earth. Is there life on this planet? We will have to wait and see.

The first exoplanet was found in 1995. More than 300 have been found since then.

Listening for Life in Space

Radio signals travel easily through space. If beings live on other planets, we may be able to hear their radio signals. Since 1960, people have been using **radio telescopes** to listen. The telescopes can pick up distant radio signals. As of 2008, no one had heard any radio signals from space, but people keep listening.

Chapter 5

Step Right Up

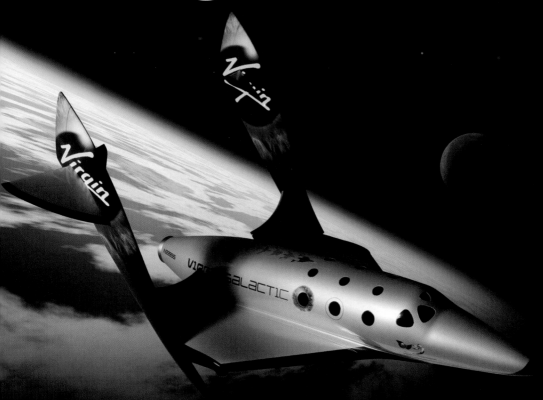

Imagine a future vacation. Instead of going to the beach, you blast off for the Moon! It sounds like a science fiction story. Yet this kind of vacation may become a reality sooner than you think!

In 2004, test pilot Michael Melvill flew *SpaceShipOne* 62.5 miles (100 km) above Earth's surface.

THE NEW SPACE RACE?

In 2001, a former astronaut named Dennis Tito became the world's first space tourist. He paid $20 million to travel on a Russian rocket to the International Space Station.

Three years later, *SpaceShipOne* became the first private craft to carry a person into space. The following year, a company started selling tickets for flights into space. The tickets cost $200,000. The company has designed and tested a new spacecraft, called *SpaceShipTwo*. It is about twice as large as *SpaceShipOne* and can carry six passengers. When will space tourists blast off? Space vacations may still be a few years away.

A Car Like a Spacecraft

In science fiction, writers have often imagined flying cars. People are not sure whether the vehicles will ever be invented. One thing is certain, however. The cars of the future will be more like spacecraft.

Voice commands: One day we may be able to tell our cars where to take us. They will follow our spoken commands.

Night vision: Computers may help us see, even if our headlights go out.

Power sources: Just like future spacecraft, cars will depend on new power sources. The vehicles might run on solar power or hydrogen power.

Sometimes, astronauts must make repairs in space. They are anchored by their feet!

AT WORK IN SPACE

Do you think you might be interested in a space-related job? You might be in luck. Not everyone can be an astronaut. Yet there are plenty of space-related jobs here on Earth, and there will be many more in the near future.

Preparing for a Job in Space Science

What is a good way to prepare for a space-related job? Look up! The night sky is a great classroom. You don't need a fancy telescope. A pair of binoculars will do the trick. Start by checking out the Moon. Take a peek at Venus and Mars. A star map will help you find them.

Most space-related jobs require math and science skills. So if you want to pursue a career in space, work hard in math and science classes.

A UNIVERSE OF JOBS

Aerospace engineers design and build spacecraft. They will be needed to create the spacecraft of the future. Other engineers will help design spacesuits and other equipment. Computer programmers will create tools that help engineers do their jobs. Computer systems experts will be needed to keep computers running well.

Experts on nutrition and medicine will be needed, too. These experts will help keep astronauts healthy during missions. Astronomers will continue to play an important role in space exploration. They will study regions of space too distant for humans to reach.

Can you picture yourself working in space?

43

AEROSPACE ENGINEER

Job Description: Design, develop, and test aircraft, spacecraft, and missiles; supervise the manufacturing of these products.

Job Outlook: Employment is expected to increase.
Earnings: $59,610 to $124,550, with a median income of $87,610

Source: Bureau of Labor Statistics

Conversation With an Aerospace Engineer

Tom Benson is an aerospace engineer. He has worked at NASA's Glenn Research Center in Cleveland, Ohio, for more than 30 years.

HOW DID YOU GET INTERESTED IN AEROSPACE?

I started by watching birds in the backyard. I envied them, because they could fly wherever they wanted to go. [I lived near an airport, and I watched] all the planes fly overhead. I built model planes and launched model rockets. I made lots of paper airplanes, too.

WHAT WAS YOUR TRAINING?

I studied aeronautical engineering [and then] went into the Air Force. I ended up helping to design airplane engines. I used my education and experience to get a job at NASA.

WHAT DO YOU DO AT YOUR JOB?

In space, there is no oxygen. So rockets carry oxygen on board.

That causes extra weight. We are trying to design rockets that could use oxygen from the atmosphere as they launch.

WHAT DO YOU LIKE ABOUT YOUR WORK?

To solve a big problem, you need to solve lots of small problems. You try something and it doesn't work, but you just keep trying. Eventually, it does work. You solve a little problem. Any time you do that, it's a great day!

WHAT ADVICE DO YOU HAVE FOR STUDENTS WHO WANT TO WORK IN AEROSPACE?

Most people think you have to be super smart at math and science to work in aerospace. You *do* have to work hard in school, but the most important thing is a positive attitude.

FIND OUT MORE

BOOKS

Scott, Elaine. *Mars and the Search for Life*. New York: Houghton Mifflin Harcourt Publishing Company, 2008.

Thinmesh, Catherine. *Team Moon: How 400,000 People Landed Apollo 11 on the Moon*. New York: Houghton Mifflin, 2006.

Way, Steve, and Gerry Bailey. *Space* (Simply Science). Pleasantville, New York: Gareth Stevens Publishing, 2009.

WEB SITES

Amazing Space
amazing-space.stsci.edu
The Space Telescope Science Institute offers explorations, homework help, and a guide to the night sky.

Earth From Space
earth.jsc.nasa.gov/sseop/efs
See how Earth looks from space. You may even be able to find your home city on this NASA site.

NASA Kids' Club
www.nasa.gov/audience/forkids/kidsclub/flash/index.html
Find games, activities, and tons of information on space exploration.

INDEX

About the Author

Gary Miller is a writer and documentary filmmaker. His interest in space began in 1969, when he watched on television as the astronauts from *Apollo 11* walked on the Moon. Gary has interviewed professional baseball players, civil rights activists, country music stars, and stock car racers. He has written on subjects from armor to zooplankton—and just about everything in between.